Network Marketing Is Dead, Long Live Network Marketing

By

Praveen Kumar & Prashant Kumar

Disclaimer

The advice contained in this material might not be suitable for everyone. The author obtained the information from sources believed to be reliable and from his own personal experience, but he neither implies nor intends any guarantee of accuracy.

The author, publisher, and distributors never give legal, accounting, medical or any other type of professional advice. The reader must always seek those services from competent professionals that can review their own particular circumstances.

The author, publisher, and distributors particularly disclaim any liability, loss, or risk taken by individuals who directly or indirectly act on the information contained herein. All readers must accept full responsibility for their use of this material.

All pictures used in this book are for illustrative purposes only. The people in the pictures are not connected with the book, author or publisher, and no link or endorsement between any of them and the topic or content is implied, nor should any be assumed. The pictures are only licensed for use in

Table of Contents

Introduction: Why Traditional Network Marketing Is Dead?

If you are struggling and making no headway in your network marketing business, then you are probably trying to build a network organization the old-fashioned way. The traditional way of building a network marketing organization is dead. It is waste of time, energy and money.

Before we start, it is important to understand the basic truth of why a majority of people fail in traditional network marketing even though it is one of the most attractive business models. People come with dreams in their eyes and leave with their hopes shattered.

Most people fail in network marketing because they have been told by their upline to Recruit, Recruit, and Recruit. For them, it is a number game. If you don't recruit, then someone else will. It is a race against time. You are told that if you recruit in large numbers then some will stick and, by the law of average, a few leaders will emerge. Most people fall prey to this myth, yet nothing can be further from the truth.

What most people don't understand is that network marketing is a **mentoring, teaching and relationship-building** business. A recruiter is interested only in numbers. The sponsor, on the other hand, takes upon himself the responsibility for the growth and welfare of the person he has sponsored. To succeed, you have to teach others to succeed. Before that, you have to learn how to succeed first.

PEOPLE WHO TREAT THEIR NETWORK AS A NUMBER NEVER SUCCEED IN THIS BUSINESS. To build a lifestyle residual business, you have to learn the art of **LEVERAGING**. Without leveraging, you will be working 80 hours a week with no results. To leverage, you have to Sponsor, Sponsor, Sponsor and then: Retain, Retain, Retain. It is better to have 5 leaders in your business who can replicate your success of teaching and mentoring others than to recruit hundreds of people who will drop out within a short span of time.

Another reason why people drop out of network marketing after the initial euphoria of dreaming about firing their boss, spending time with their family and travelling around the world wears off is because they find that creating a sustainable network is incredibly hard. They have to make appointments, do 3- way calls, drive around and make presentations every night after a tiring day at work. On weekends, there are presentations by the leaders and you have to virtually drag your prospects to attend. On many occasions, you find yourself stranded because the prospect does not turn up for the presentation and doesn't even have the courtesy to inform you. Then there are product training seminars. These presentations cost time, effort and money.

It does not stop here. To succeed in this business, you have to build relationships with your prospects. Training and mentoring your team is immensely time-consuming. You need effort and knowledge to develop leadership within your organization in order to create a sustainable network.

Building a sustainable organization requires a huge amount of physical and mental energy. When starting out, most people are doing it on a part-time basis. After a day's hard work, they have to spend time away from their family to build their network marketing business. This is definitely not what they bargained for when they joined the business. You can't call this a lifestyle business. Instead of spending time with their family and following their dreams they are now caught in a life of daily drudgery.

Difference between Growth and Maintenance

Most people joining a network marketing business do not understand the difference between the growth and maintenance aspect of a business. Growth is when you are exploring new avenues of business or expanding your existing business. Maintenance is the time spent on sustaining your existing business. If the business you join is very high maintenance in terms of time, cost and effort then your growth will suffer. This is not good for your financial or physical health. To grow, you need more time and freedom to explore new thoughts and ideas.

By joining low maintenance business opportunities you give yourself a chance to join more than one network marketing company and create multiple streams of residual income. In today's uncertain times, it is very important to create multiple streams of income. It eliminates the risk. Even your job is not secure these days, as many have learned during these hard times. If the maintenance aspect of a business is high, then you will find it extremely hard to join more than one business. **To succeed, you have to join business**

opportunities that offer a very high growth with very low maintenance.

Retention Rate

The retention rate of affiliates in a majority of network marketing companies ranges between 8 to 15%. You keep sponsoring new affiliates whilst the old ones keep dropping out. It is an endless process and your effort never ceases. It is simply too hard to build a sustainable network with such high dropout rates. Luckily, there are business opportunities that have retention rates in excess of 70%. If you can find and join these companies then your effort in building your network becomes extremely easy.

Cash Flow

When most affiliates join network marketing business, they are attracted by the residual earning aspect of the business. This is great because residual income is very important. What most people fail to understand is the importance of cash flow. **It is cash flow that pays your bills and gives you lifestyle. Cash flow also pays the cost of running your business. Without cash flow, you cannot sustain or expand your business.** Business expansion requires marketing, which needs loads of money. No one can sustain a business which is only supported by money out of their pockets. It starts to hurt. No wonder most people drop out after a few months.

So the key to success in network marketing is to find businesses that not only give you residual income in the long term as you build your network but also give the high cash flow needed to sustain and grow your business. **Without cash flow, your business will die.**

It is strange that people join network marketing businesses where companies pay only 5- 25% of the profits depending upon the rank achieved by the affiliate. **A new affiliate only earns at the lower end of the scale which is normally less than 10% commission. Can anyone sustain his business with such a pittance of payments?** After a few months of paying out of their pockets, most affiliates drop out. I simply cannot blame them because a business is supposed to pay you and not have you shell out your hard earned money to sustain your business. This is a recipe for failure.

Fortunately, there are **companies that are willing to pay you exceedingly well (30-50% commissions) for your effort in promoting their products and services**. If you join such companies, you generate huge cash flow within days of joining the business. You also reach break-even point and recoup your initial investment within days if not months of joining the business. Once you recover your initial investment you become risk-free.

Positioning

Why is it that some people are able to sponsor hundreds of affiliates into the network marketing business while others find it hard to sponsor even one person into their organization? The secret lies in 'Positioning'. To succeed in network marketing, you have to **position yourself as a LEADER** so that prospects gravitate towards you. Once you are perceived as a leader, you will never have to chase anyone to join your business; people will start chasing you to join your organization. This is the secret of a successful network marketer.

The challenge is how to position yourself as a leader when you are starting out in your business. Because most people lack credibility they fall back on the easy option of borrowing credibility of their upline leadership. They promote their upline leaders instead of themselves. As a result, success eludes them even further.

Internet and Business Systems: Long Live Internet Marketing

The internet has changed the rules of the game. The traditional style of network marketing is dead. It is simply too hard and does not work for over 90% of the prospects who join the business and then drop out. The new generation of network marketers is internet savvy and can create lifestyle income with minimum time and effort.

It is now possible to **build very large networks within a very short period of time using the internet**. It is possible to automate the whole process of lead generation, training, relationship building and leadership training by using the correct systems. You can work in your pyjamas and never call a prospect. The principles of network marketing have not changed. The internet has changed the method of doing business which is now effortless and simplified.

Then why are affiliates still struggling while most companies have websites to promote their business? Unfortunately, most of the internet marketing companies have not figured out how business is conducted on the internet. Most companies give you an affiliate link with a fancy video about the state of the economy and how selling their innovative product will help you escape the rat race and fulfil your dreams of driving a Ferrari or owning a beach house. They think that by simply giving an affiliate some website with a fancy video, they will help you create a successful online business.

We all fall prey to these slick video presentations and join a business opportunity without any analysis. What happens thereafter? Most people don't know how to drive traffic to the replicated landing page which thousands of others are promoting on the internet. They have no marketing plan, strategy or sales funnel. In frustration, they fall back upon the warm market and it is the same old drudgery of showing the plan and 3-way telephone calls with their sponsor.

Building a network marketing business on the internet is an exact science. Not every MLM product or company is suited for the internet business. Most people join the wrong company and promote products that are not suited for marketing on the internet.

This book will show you the right method of building a successful online network marketing business. It will teach you the right way to leverage your time, effort and money.

By learning the principles in this book you will be able to create multiple streams of residual income with minimum effort. If you are to succeed in network marketing, you will need a system. Every successful business is built around a system. If you look at every successful network marketer who has built an organization, you will find a system that can be duplicated easily by the team. The secret to your success lies in the system.

Without a system, there is no leveraging and without leveraging there is no lifestyle business. If you are serious about succeeding in the network marketing business, then you will need a system. Without a system, you will be wasting your time, energy and frustrating yourself.

This book will show you how you can use technology to:

- Position yourself as a leader in the network marketing niche

- Use a viral blogging platform to generate free traffic to your website and capture leads

- Create a perpetual sales funnel to generate qualified leads into your business

- Build systems for mentoring and relationship making which is critical to your building a successful and sustainable network.

- Make a home office business and communication centre where you can monitor every aspect of your business.

Architecture Of A Lifestyle Business

- Most people join network marketing business with dreams of a fancy lifestyle but without the proper understanding of what it takes to succeed in this business.

- They are lured into joining after seeing a slick presentation or being persuaded by friends and family who themselves do not have any clear idea about what they are doing. It is like the blind leading the blind. Because they join for all the wrong reasons, they get disillusioned and quit when they don't see any tangible results for their effort.

- The most important thing about any business is that it must have huge *Cash Flow*. It is the cash flow that pays your bills and gives you a lifestyle. If you have cash flow, your business will grow and thrive. If you don't have cash flow, your business will collapse.

- Traditional network marketing companies that sell **Physical Products** such as vitamins, juices, cosmetics, soaps and other household items give a commission of **5% to 25%** to their affiliates, depending on the qualification level. On the other hand, Digital Product companies that sell information and entertainment products generally distribute **30% to 50%** of the profits and at times higher to their affiliates. They can afford to pay such high commissions because, after the initial development cost, there are no further manufacturing, warehousing or distribution costs.

- Another advantage of a Digital Product is that it can be **Delivered Instantaneously**. In today's world of instant gratification, this is a huge plus point.

- Digital products can also be sold to customers around the globe. The whole world is your oyster. In the case of physical products, the parent company has to take approvals from the local governments and set up infrastructure such as warehousing and distribution channels before they can launch into a new market.

- If a new country opens up for business, you will need to physically travel to that country to launch your business in that country. This will cost you time, effort and money.

- Most physical products have **Safety Issues**. These products need to be demonstrated to new customers and affiliates for proper usage. This requires time-consuming **Training and Hard Work**.

For this reason, most physical product companies will not allow you to start a blog or website to market your business. They fear misrepresentation of their products. You are only allowed to promote the company affiliate website which takes the sting out of your eCommerce marketing effort as hundreds of thousands of other affiliates are promoting the same website and you simply cannot stand out.

Digital products have **No Safety Issues**. Most internet- based companies understand eCommerce and help you in your effort to market the product globally. It is possible for you to build websites selling digital products. This forms the basis of a lifestyle business that can make **Auto**

Sales without your intervention, once set up correctly.

Another important thing is the **Retention** of affiliates. There is no point in joining a company that has very poor retention rate. Your hard work will put to waste if a very high percentage of the prospects you sponsor into the business drop out soon after.

Historically, physical product companies have an average retention rate of around 8%. If you are an outstanding leader with great support and training program then your retention rate can go up to 10% to 15%. To build a network with such a high attrition rate will entail extreme persistence and hard work.

If you are to earn a lifestyle income then your Retention Rates have to be close to **100%**. Your business should be compact so that affiliates don't drop out. This is possible if the affiliates you sponsor start making money within days if not months of joining the business opportunity.

No one will drop out of your organization if they start seeing cash flow and are in profit after having recovered their initial investment.

There are several innovative companies on the internet that recognize the fact that many new affiliates are not professional marketers and find it difficult to sponsor new prospects into the business.

To improve the retention rate, they offer **Profit Share** so that new affiliates who join the business start to earn money even if they do not sponsor a single person into the business.

Once a new affiliate makes money, it becomes easy for them to sponsor others into the business with confidence because their **Belief in the Business** goes up. It reflects in their body language when they speak with new prospects.

Businesses that work well are those that pay their affiliates high revenue share. By making just two to three sales, an affiliate recovers the initial investment. After having reached the breakeven point with the first sale, can you think of any reason why the affiliate would drop out of the business?

If you are to create a sustained lifestyle and long-term wealth, then cash flow by itself is not sufficient. The business you join must unleash steady flow of **Residual Income** that will last for years. Smart businesses are those that create not only cash flow but also residual income quickly.

A lifestyle business is only possible if you can apply **Leverage** that can reduce your time and effort. All large sums of money embrace the generalized principle of leverage. Big doors swing on little hinges.

Without leverage, you will not be able to maximize your income or free up your time to pursue your dreams. You need *Technology* and *Business Systems* to provide you the leverage. Every successful business has systems in place and so should you. Without proper systems, you will work like a mule all your life. Systems give you leverage to enjoy a lifestyle business.

The business you join must embrace the principle of **SIMPLICITY**. The business itself can be complex but must be very simple to operate on a day-to-day basis. This is why franchises like McDonald's work very well- because of their simplicity. They can be manned by unskilled staff and part-time student workers anywhere in the world.

Lastly, and most importantly, the highest leverage you can apply in your business is by choosing the **Right Team** to join. A professional team will provide you with the *Support, Training* and *Systems* that will guarantee not only your success but also of the prospects that join your organization.

It is easy to comprehend the architecture of a lifestyle business but relatively complex to find an ideal company that will satisfy all the criteria we have discussed. In the next chapter, we will discuss **How to find Lifestyle Business Opportunities** that give you Cash Flow and Residual Income.

How to Analyse and Find the Right Company to Join

Internet is the new gold rush with a promise to create a large amount of wealth within a very short time span. There are many unscrupulous companies that are on the lookout to make you part with your hard earned money.

You are bombarded with emails and offers of new business opportunities every day. It can be very confusing because some of the video presentations are slick and deliver powerful emotional content. They create scarcity and time deadlines to force you to act without thinking.

You have to be very careful about jumping at the opportunity without understanding the risks. It is important to carry out a dispassionate analysis before joining. It is not only your money that is involved but also your invaluable time and effort.

The first step is to analyse the business concept of the company. Find out: *How does the Business Earn Money*? The company can share revenues with you only if they make money. This is the first test the company should pass.

Does the internet company have a registered office? *A Physical Address* is very important. Most internet companies operate without a physical address. They should be registered in a country where there are strong compliance laws. Avoid companies that are registered in a banana republic or a small Pacific island that no one has heard of. If possible, you or someone you trust should visit the physical office to check if the company really exists.

You should know who the *Promoters* of the company are. The names of the promoters and directors must be public. You should research the background of the promoters to check their business and integrity record. The promoters should not be hiding behind a website but be accessible to affiliates to meet and interact.

It is important that the company you join has a *Track Record* of successful business operations. Avoid new start-ups because the failure rate is simply too high.

The Company you choose must have a *Strong Compliance* department. Compliance is irksome but essential for survivability of the company. A good criterion is to join companies that are registered in first world countries. Such businesses will have to operate under strict compliance.

The business opportunity you promote must **Compensate Handsomely** for the work you put in. There are companies that pay you a pittance. You should avoid them. Join companies that pay affiliates in **excess of 30%** of the company profits. You will struggle with anything less.

Join companies selling **Big Ticket Items**. Time and effort for making a $10 commission is the same as making $1000 commission.

Selling higher value items also allows you to increase your marketing budget. It is an excellent strategy to work with companies that have a low value item for sale upfront but have high value items for sale at the back end. This allows a prospect to sign up for a lower value program and upgrade at a later date.

The Company must have a strong record of **Paying on Time**. Delayed payments are the first sign of trouble that the company has cash flow problems.

The business opportunity should provide you with **Leverage**. The internet has become the biggest marketplace for direct selling. Every company wants to reward you in some way to sell their products. The company you join should have business systems to help their affiliates and encourage selling their products through the internet.

Before jumping into an opportunity, you must check out **How you Get Paid**. Avoid companies that do not pay through legitimate payment processors. Avoid companies that are not a credit card or PayPal approved. The compensation plan must not only provide you with cash flow but also residual income.

Cash flow is important to run your day-to-day business. Leverage, on the other hand, provides you with the opportunity of creating residual income. **Residual Income** means that you earn income regardless of what you do this week, working or not.

Join a company that provides **Innovation**. In today's technology-driven world only companies that innovate will survive. There are so many business models that are just copies of others, they don't offer innovation.

Companies that do not have innovation will not survive for long. Your effort in working with these companies will come to naught. Positioning yourself in an innovation-structured business model that allows you to benefit from the upscale and upward growth will greatly enhance your chances of success.

How to Minimize Your Risk in the Network Marketing Industry

Most prospects focus on rewards when joining a network marketing opportunity because of the marketing hype. Video presentation is prepared by copywriters who are masters at triggering our impulsive buying emotion, but the risks of the business proposition are never discussed.

To take cognizance of the risks is important because every business opportunity carries with it an element of risk. If you are to succeed in your business venture, you have to learn how to manage risks that are part and parcel of any business enterprise.

The first step is to passionately **_Analyse the Company_** that you are joining. It is important to check the track record of the company, the people behind the business & their track records.

You must also analyse the business concepts and how they earn their profits. The company can share revenues with you, only if they make money.

The company you choose must also be strong on compliance or they will be shut down by the authorities. You minimize your risk by joining the right business opportunity.

Rapid advances in technology have shortened the **Life Cycle of Products**. New breakthroughs can make the products of the company which you are marketing redundant.

Remember Kodak? This company was a market leader in photo films at the turn of the century. Today, the company has gone into liquidation state because digital cameras made photo films redundant.

The reality is that every product has a life cycle. The trick is to find innovative companies that adjust to the market conditions and add new product lines to their mix.

Generally speaking, more the rewards, the higher the risks involved. This should not dissuade you from joining a high reward company if your aim is to create wealth quickly. What you have to put in place is **Risk Management Strategies** to mitigate the risks.

A good strategy is to **Recoup Your Initial Investment** within the shortest possible time frame. You should earn profit within months if not in days. The pace of technology had compressed the product life cycles. It also generates much higher profits within limited time frame.

Higher profits enable you to be in profit within a very short period of time. You have to work with companies that give you cash flow to recover your initial investment within a very short time frame.

Most affiliates have the tendency to start slowly, testing the waters and then increase the size of their investment and commitment to a program. The problem with this approach is that your risk period extends with each incremental investment and upgrade you make.

A better strategy is to first analyse the business opportunity, and if you decide to join, then start with the highest level of investment that your budget will allow. By doing so, you keep your risk period down to the minimum.

Another strategy is to **Spread your Risk**. You have to _Create Multiple Streams of Residual Income_ to survive in today's world. The rich people do not depend on only one source of income, but grow orchards of "money trees." If one source of income disappears, your lifestyle will not be affected as you have other sources of residual income to support you.

How to Create Multiple Streams of Residual Income on the Internet

Prosperous people are always aware that if one stream of income dries up, they have many more to tap into for support. Ordinary folks are much more vulnerable. If they lose one of their streams, it wipes them out.

In this fast-changing, uncertain world, you need a portfolio of residual income streams from completely different and diversified sources. If one stream empties, you'll barely notice. You'll be stable. You will have time to adjust. You will be safe.

The key to wealth and happiness in today's world is to create multiple streams of income using diverse models that give you a combination of high **Cash Flow** and **Residual Income**.

Cash Flow will support your lifestyle and pay your bills. **Residual Income** will build long-term wealth.

The concept of creating financial security through multiple streams of residual income is very appealing. You diversify your investment and business risks; however, the problem lies in its implementation.

Instead of creating a relaxed lifestyle, you can get sucked into a situation where you have to become hyperactive in trying to control and maintain your residual income sources.

Financial success comes from focused attention to one specific outcome. The effort in creating multiple streams of income diffuses your focus and creates extraordinary demands of your limited time. It can cause undue strain and stress in your life.

Your chances of failure increase in proportion to your diffused focus. In order to succeed in creating multiple streams of residual income, you have to learn to reconcile two seemingly contradictory realities of how to focus and also create multiple streams of income at the same time.

There is also a need to balance our family, health, relationships, recreation and spiritual needs. Happiness lies in balancing our needs correctly rather than focusing only on one aspect of life. Financial security is extremely important, but it must not be allowed to dominate every aspect of our lives.

The right way to create multiple streams of income is to focus on building **One Business Stream** first.

Once you have created your first income stream, you must _automate your income stream_ so that it does not require intervention on a day-to-day basis. There will be some maintenance required, but if you put the proper systems into place, then the time required for maintenance can be minimized. You will need to invest in the right systems and technology to automate your business.

Once your first business is in profit, you will need to _leverage your income from this opportunity to create additional streams of residual income_. Your first income stream is the most important one because you are going to leverage your knowledge and resources from this business to build other income streams.

The second income stream is just the **Repeat Process** of the first one. You can now make improvements based on your experience in creating the first income stream. You will also need lesser time, effort and money because of your experience. The return from the second income stream normally is a lot higher than the first venture.)

Once you hit on a successful residual income formula, just keep refining and repeating it. Creating residual income can, at times, be a very boring process. The money part though, is of course very exciting.

Be warned... the human mind wants excitement. It will ask you to try out new ventures and divert your resources. You have to resist this temptation and keep focused on repeating and maximizing your success formula.

You have to understand the difference between **Maintenance Work** and **Growth Work**. There is no such thing as totally passive income. Every passive income will have some maintenance work.

It may not require your day to day involvement, but monitoring work will be needed. Even as you carry out maintenance work you should be on the lookout for new growth opportunities. Growth work creates multiple income streams.

You should focus on one growth opportunity at a time. Create a successful residual income from it before moving on to another growth activity. You will make money efficiently by following this simple strategy without overwhelming yourself.

Not all residual income streams are equal. Some may require more maintenance effort than others. If you _have to create multiple residual income streams, you have to find the business opportunities that require the least maintenance work_.

The internet is perhaps the easiest way to create multiple streams of income with the least effort. This is because you can automate the process of lead capture, building relationships, making sales as well as giving product and marketing training. In addition, you can make multiple sales to the same lead.

How to Attract Free Targeted Traffic to Your Website

Driving web traffic to the business opportunity that you are promoting is the key to your success on the internet. Without traffic, there is no business.

The key to getting targeted traffic to your website is to **Position Yourself as a Knowledge Leader** in your niche so that people want your knowledge and start following you.

Positioning yourself as a leader is as easy as ABC.

1.You have to become an expert in your field. To do that, you always have to be a student. Willingness to learn will make you an expert.

2.You need to share the knowledge that you have gained with your prospects. When you start to add value to others, they will start following you.

3.The final step is to share your story and personal results. Sharing your story creates an emotional attachment and people start relating to you at a personal level.

I will now show you some easy action steps on how to prove that you are an expert in your niche.

- **Share your Philosophy**. You have to state your point of view and show how it is different from others in your niche. If you can stand out from the crowd and show your personality, then you will attract followers. Your philosophy will make people think and gravitate towards you.

- **Tell People about your Popularity**. Speak of your achievements in your niche. How many website hits you have? Talk about your video that went viral. Talk about your success.

- **Give Yourself a Title**. People respect you for your title. You can be the CEO, VP or Director of your internet business.

- **Borrow Credibility from your Upline Leadership**. This will be a source of inspiration to others who are planning to join you. They will be excited to join a great organization.

- **Get Testimonials from Credible Partners**. Ask your upline leaders. They will give you testimonials to build your credibility.

- **Increase your Visibility**. As a leader, you have to increase your visibility. Any press release is good exposure. Write articles, books or appear on television. Be a guest speaker or a guest on another blog.

- **Give Social Proof**. Talk about people who have joined your group and how you helped them. If you are just starting out, then borrow credibility from the success of your team or your business systems.

- **Create Products**. If you have products for sale, then it will put you on a completely different level. A perfect example is if you write a book about your niche, it gives the impression that you are a professional.

- **Tell your Story**. Share your story on how you struggled and figured it all out. People love to hear stories, especially the 'rags-to-riches' types. If you can show how you solved a particular problem then people with a similar issue will start to follow you.

Reverse Marketing

Reverse Marketing occurs when prospects start calling and wanting to join your team rather than you calling the prospects. Prospects will gravitate towards you when they feel that you have the solution to their problems and they can gain something from you. There is a pull towards you when prospects see the possibility of enlightenment by associating with you.

Reverse marketing is about building relationships and being viewed by your prospects as someone who can help them solve their problems. When this happens, you become more valuable to them. It takes very little time for people to form an impression of someone they just met and that impression tends to stick, so it is very important that you make the right impression.

You have to position yourself as a knowledgeable and credible leader to make reverse marketing effective. You have to show your potential prospects that you are living their ideal lifestyle. This will pique their curiosity and have them wanting to know how you did it.

- This is essential in branding you as the mentor in the mind of the prospect. It is important to remember that as a role model you need to maintain a _strong character and ethics_. By demonstrating that you are sincere, safe and trustworthy you can create a lasting rapport within 90 seconds.

You have to *play hard to get*. The key step is to preserve your image and project that your time is valuable to the prospect. If you position yourself as someone being sought after, people will value and respect you.

If you beg for prospects' attention, it will devalue your position as a sought-after leader. If you make yourself scarce, then it will give you an upper hand in the relationship.

The last step in the process of reverse marketing is to give your prospects a chance to join you by *opening a small window of opportunity*. This is a crucial step. A perfect example will be to send out an email to your list letting them know that you have an opening in your schedule to work with two people and ask them why they should be selected. This step will eliminate time wasters and bring serious prospects to the foreground.

How to Convert Traffic into Leads and Build Relationships on Auto-Pilot

To convert traffic into leads and build relations on auto-pilot is a very simple 4 step process.

- The first step you need to do is to find a problem that everyone has in your niche.

- The second one is to build a lead capture page with an offer to solve the problem. This will entice people to fill out the form.

- Third is to tell them exactly how to solve the problem.

- And lastly is to build a relationship with your leads by giving follow-up information.

For example, in building the lead capture page for the network marketing sales funnel, you should focus on the fact that over 90% of the prospects who joined the network marketing opportunities fail to make money and normally quit within 6 months of joining the business. They have no understanding on what types of businesses succeed on the internet, how to position themselves as leaders and how to leverage the power of the internet.

In the squeeze page, _you should sell the results and not the product_. The result in this case, can be showing your would-be prospects on how to become successful network marketers and earn a lifestyle income by positioning themselves as leaders by using proven business systems.

You should not try and sell a business opportunity at the beginning because you do not have a relationship with the prospect at this stage. It takes time to develop relationships.

Once a person fills out the form, they start to follow you. The next stage is to build a relationship of trust through follow up emails or videos. It takes several points of contact to build a relationship.

At this stage, you must focus on their problem and give them solutions with demonstrable results. Once they can visualize the results, the task of selling a solution becomes very simple.

Let us look at another example. If you are selling gym equipment, you will fail if you start focusing on the features like how strong the construction is, what the horsepower is or how reliable the machine is.

This information is important, but it does not focus on the results which the client is seeking. Your client has a problem with his body. You will succeed if you tell the prospect how chiselled and toned the body will become after using the machine. *You have to sell the results and not the features to gain attention.*

The next step is to convert the leads into loyal followers. This is a very crucial step. You cannot ask someone to purchase the product without gaining their respect and trust.

You have to deliver on the promised result. This is where most people fail. They fail to deliver and build relationships. To gain loyal followers, you have to deliver on the **Promised Results**.

We know that people don't like to be sold. If you try and sell something, people become defensive and put up 'The Wall'. So how do you avoid the wall?

You avoid the wall by *shifting your focus from selling towards helping people with their problem*. You avoid the solution you are trying to sell. The solution is automatic once you have helped them come to the conclusion of what they need to do to solve their problem.

Another important point is that you need to help people realize that they need help. Don't force your help to them.

The reason why most people don't use this approach is that it takes a lot of time and effort to educate people with regards to their own problem. There is also the possibility of no result after a huge amount of effort.

This is why only big ticket sellers such as real estate agents adopt this strategy. They give their clients all the information and education because even one sale out of five will cover the costs of their time and effort.

Will this strategy work for low ticket items? Is it worth the effort in network marketing to educate potential clients about their problems when the conversion rates are well below 10%? Do you have the energy needed to follow up with your clients?

It takes several days and calls to make a sale after building a relationship of trust. The good news is, technology allows us to automate the process of educating a client by using a **Marketing Sales Funnel**.

Once a lead has been captured, you can send a series of educational emails and videos to build relationships automatically. This turns cold leads into followers that know, like and trust you. This is because you just helped them solve their problem, which was causing them a great deal of pain.

Auto Sales: How to Convert Followers into Buyers Without Calling Anyone

The way to convert followers into buyers without selling or picking up the phone is by using a ***video sales presentation*** that is digitally delivered online. A long winding text or sales letter does not convert well. A video sales presentation, on the other hand, presents your product and call-to-purchase more effectively.

A video sales letter is like a presentation you are making to a live audience. The only difference is that it is delivered electronically. You are replicating a sales representative, without ever having to pay a dime. This provides you with a huge leverage in terms of auto sales.

All you need is a state-of-the-art autoresponder that captures leads, builds auto relationships through education and delivers a video sales letter once the client is convinced the solution you are offering is the right one.

The next thing you need, when you call-to-action, is an *e-commerce system that allows you to accept payments directly to your bank account*.

The next phase of auto sales is to be able to make money from your buyers month- after- month on an autopilot. To do that, you need to sell **continuity programs** that pay you monthly commissions for a sale made once. This creates a residual income stream for you.

There is no point in selling items that give you cash for a one-time sale. You cannot create a sustainable business with one-time sale products.

Not all continuity programs are successful. Some people like to promote membership sites. A membership site needs to provide tremendous value month-after-month to sustain the membership.

It is our experience that most membership sites fail to deliver after few months, and clients tend to drop out after they have received the information they were seeking. Most membership sites also pay you only at one level deep. This does not create a sustainable residual income because there is no leveraging by the members you sponsor.

By far, the best solution is to _promote companies that sell digital products through network marketing model_ on the internet. This creates residual income as it leverages the team effort with the power of the internet.

The trick is to find companies that can pay you a high cash flow for each sale and reward you with a great residual income potential if you build a large network organization. It is advisable to promote well-thought programs with high retention rates.

The next step of auto-monetization is to **increase your income per lead without calling or selling**.

If you had successfully created a network marketing organization for selling one product or service, then it is very easy to sell another product or service to the same network because they understand the necessity of creating multiple streams of residual income.

The best part is that you don't even have to train them again because they are fully educated about building a network.

The last part of the auto-monetization process is to **offer time-saving solutions** to the members of your network marketing team. Products that you offer must make their lives easier in order to accomplish their goals. You must first be sold on the product yourself before recommending it to your team.

Your love of the product can earn you commissions by recommending it to your team. If the product you sell creates a residual income for your team and also adds to their efficiency, then it is an absolute win-win situation for everyone.

Having more products and services available for purchase to your team will earn you more money on every lead you capture. There is, however, a word of caution. To succeed long-term, the products that you sell must help your team achieve their goals and make them successful.

If you try and sell products that are of no value to your team and just to line up your pocket, then your organization will lose faith in your integrity and judgment. This is the first step towards disintegrating your organization. ***Ethics and integrity*** behind auto sales is very important. You may never meet or see a client, but you have to treat them with great care and respect.

Duplication: How to Gain Massive Leverage by Duplicating the Automated Process for Your Team

Duplication is the most important piece to a successful network marketing system. No matter what business you are in, or what products you are selling, it is very important to make sure that your team duplicates your success model.

Duplication is the fundamental principle to building a successful network marketing organization that will sustain the test of time. Without the help of a successful duplicating system, your effort in building a network will never cease. You will never have a lifestyle business.

Have you ever wondered why a Big Mac and Fries at McDonald's always tastes the same, no matter where you are in the world? Or why every McDonald franchise is always successful wherever it opens? It is not luck, rather a series of processes that have been perfected over the years.

McDonald's has a system in place that duplicates their practices, and processes across every country, every restaurant and every employee that they have for consistency.

By duplicating the success model that worked for them over the years, McDonald's Corporation can open a new location and be confident that it will yield successful results.

If you apply the same strategy in your network marketing business, then you and any prospect that joins your organization will be guaranteed of success. In order to achieve true duplication, the system that you will need must have the following 6 factors.

Simplicity

The most important feature that your system must have is ***SIMPLICITY***. You must have a push button system that is easy to use with minimal training. The system must be user- friendly so that masses can use it without difficulty.

It can be driven by sophisticated technology but must have a user-friendly interface so that a totally, non-technical person can operate it with ease and be successful. It must be like a high-tech car that is easy to drive.

Structure

The duplicating system must have a *structure* that prospects can follow. It is very important to have a proper set of procedures and a rock solid game plan built into the system. You will be a winner if the plan is an easy to follow step-by-step roadmap to success which your prospects can follow without difficulty.

Comprehensive

The *Duplicating Plan* must be comprehensive. It must _duplicate the lead capture pages, sales funnel, traffic generation, presentations, follow up and monetization._ If you have all these elements in place, then you will arm your members with a system which is built for them to succeed.

Quick to Setup

The system must be *quick to set up*. Most people who join a network marketing company are first-timers. By creating an effective step-by-step "getting started" process for new recruits, you will find that you will spend less time hand-holding and more time enrolling. The system must be technology-driven in order to give you true leverage.

Training

"*If you give a man a fish, he will eat for a day. If you teach a man to fish, he will eat for a lifetime*". People are always learning at all aspects of their life and in business.

By having a training system with documents, audios, videos and webinars, you will find that you will keep your organization educated, informed and on track.

Training is the key to the success of your organization. Training develops leadership and helps in relationship-building. The better the training, the faster your business and your team members will grow.

A good training system must not only be duplicable but must also pass 100% of the information to the new prospects to succeed. Training cannot be left to chance where there is loss of information in the system.

For example, let's say that Tom sponsors Peter. Even if Tom is a great teacher and tries to impart training, there is loss of information. The amount of loss will depend upon the communication skills of Tom and the receptivity level of Peter. Similarly, when Peter tries to teach his prospect

Charles about the business, there is further loss of information.

Duplication system cannot rely on the individual's training skill levels of their members. Every member of the team must be taught skills directly by an expert.

It is surprising that a majority of network marketing companies still rely on the individual skills of their members to impart product and marketing training. This is a recipe for disaster.

A technology-driven training system based on videos, audios and webinars, can ensure that there is no loss of information within the system.

Problem with Replicated Websites

Duplication is fine but in the world of internet marketing, Google and other search engines do not like replication. Most network marketing companies give you a replicate website with a fancy presentation of their business opportunity.

The problem is ***Google does not like replicate websites and penalizes these websites***. Replicated websites do not come up in the search results and get no free traffic.

Google and Facebook do not even allow paid advertisements using replicated websites. They consider replicate websites poor on user experience and equivalent to spamming with hundreds and thousands of affiliates trying to promote the same website.

Most affiliates find it extremely difficult to drive free or paid traffic to these replicated websites. Remember- *without traffic there is no business*. This is the cause of failure of most internet based MLM businesses.

Viral Blogging Platform

You can solve this problem by integrating a viral blogging platform with your sales funnel. By blogging, your website becomes content-driven. It now has a distinct signature that Google and other search engines love. In addition, your website should be fully integrated with social media including Facebook, Twitter, Pinterest, Google+ etc. If someone comments on your articles or clicks on the 'Like' button, it shows up on their Facebook page for their friends to see and comment. This drives even more traffic to your website, and your article gets more comments and exposure. As a result, your traffic goes viral.

The Eight Principles of a Successful Network Marketing Plan

Let us look at some of the principles that you need to incorporate to become a successful internet marketer. Without following these principles, there is virtually no possibility to succeed with your network marketing business.

 # Constant Targeted Traffic to Your Website. You have to get constant targeted traffic to your website. If there is no traffic, there is no business. You can have the best business; marketing funnel and lead capture pages but if you have no traffic, then nothing will convert. Period.

 # Viral and Converting Website. As discussed earlier, your website must have a system with a marketing funnel, lead capture pages and a viral blogging platform that can be replicated by your entire team. The system should be designed to attract the most qualified new leads into your business.

 # Convert Leads into Sales. The system should have professionally produced videos and written emails that are designed to build relationships with prospects without you having to call them. It should convert leads into buyers even while you sleep. A video sales letter works better than emails to build relationship with prospects.

Attract Motivated Entrepreneurs. Use your website to position yourself as a knowledgeable leader so that people naturally want to follow you, with a credit card in hand and ready to join whichever business you want to show them. In essence, you become an expert and your prospects seek your attention.

Eliminate Time-Wasters. Design a good sales funnel using leading network marketing software technology which literally divides and conquers your leads and eliminates time- wasters so that you only interact with the most qualified leads who are interested in joining you.

Earn More Money. Whether it's to grow your business faster or just enjoy life, your system should have multiple revenue streams that generate cash flow and also build residual income streams to create long term wealth. Your system should be designed to generate more income per lead.

 # Simplify and Automate. With existing technologies, you can build a business system that not only attracts new leads but also converts them into sales for your business. The system you designed should be able to automate the daily tasks of relationship-building, follow-up and training.

 # Duplicate it for Your Team. The system you designed must be 100% duplicable by your downline. Your new distributors should be up and running in seconds. Hand-holding is a thing of the past with new internet technology.

The system you designed must teach, inspire and lead each member of your team to succeed with a simple step-by step-plan using easy-to-follow instructions. If your team members succeed, so will you.

In brief:

- To succeed on the internet, you need a system that will help project you as a leader.

- You need a system that allows you to deliver your message and share it with the world. There is no point in having a message that no one reads.

- You need a system that spreads your message virally using social media.

- You need a system that lets complete strangers find your reports on Google and start to follow you. Your loyal followers will make your information go viral on the internet.

- You need a system that duplicates your team effort and guarantees every member of your team success. Your success lies in their successes.

- It is important to have a system that promotes you as market leader in your niche and automates all the business processes. Such a system will provide you the leverage for a successful lifestyle business.

Of equal importance is the type of businesses you plug into the system to make it a success. Most people fail because they plug in the wrong business to the system and then blame the system. If the two don't match up, then the wealth-building system will simply not work.

What are the Types of Network Marketing Businesses that Work with Automated Business Systems?

You can have the best marketing and duplication system but if you choose the wrong business to plug into the system, then the result will be one big disaster. Most people will blame the system, but the problem actually is the business.

Most people who join the network marketing business are doing it for the first time. They have no business background or understanding of what it costs to run a business.

The majority of people out there will tell you that the only money you need is to invest in is the registration cost, buy the products, use them and recommend them to others. That is far from the truth.

In running any business successfully, you will need a start-up capital and some money to cover the cost of running and promoting the business.

When joining a business, most people do not budget the running costs. They only look at the initial purchase price of the product or business. *Factoring the cost of running a business is critical to your success.*

I agree that the start-up cost for a network business is extremely low compared to the traditional business because you work from home.

One of the most important running costs that you need to consider is the marketing budget. *Promotion is crucial to the success of your business.* It is critical on how much money you spend towards promoting your business. Each dollar spent in promotion must have a tangible outcome for your business or you will go bust.

There are two critical parts of any business plan. First is to *generate cash flow to pay for the promotional and running cost of your business*. You cannot sustain a business with money coming out of your pocket.

The second important thing is to *recover your initial investment within the shortest possible time* frame so that business from that point onwards becomes risk-free.

Most people who join business opportunities have very little or no cash flow. Some businesses have incredibly high-maintenance costs in terms of effort and time spent in running their businesses, hence they have no room for growth and expansion.

The best test for finding a good business opportunity is to check what _percentage of the profit the parent company is paying out to their affiliates_. If this percentage is less than 35% then simply stay away.

The second test to _find out how many affiliates you will need to sponsor, in order to meet your operating costs._

There are business opportunities that don't require you to sponsor even one person to generate a healthy cash flow. These are called profit-share opportunities. In recent years, such income opportunities have become high-risk. There are also businesses that offer 30 to 50% commissions. If you make two to three sales, then you recover your initial investment and meet the running cost of your business. Businesses with which you can recover your initial investment within weeks/ months are very sticky with very high retention rates. Who will leave a business that is making money?

We also find that most people do not have the time, knowledge or skill to analyse a business opportunity. They joined a business opportunity because they were swayed by a fancy presentation or through pressure from family and friends.

To succeed, you have *to join a company that offers a huge cash flow and also builds residual income rapidly*. You have to carry out breakeven analysis and risk management. In addition, all businesses are not suited to being promoted efficiently on the internet. To succeed, you have to weigh and measure several different elements before joining a business opportunity.

It is a tall task for anyone who is starting out on a journey to build an online business. They simply do not have the knowledge or skills. No wonder so many people fail to make a dime or are lured by unscrupulous people in parting with their hard-earned money.

There is no point in offering a state-of-the-art marketing and duplication system and then allowing affiliates to plug in a business opportunity of their choice. This is simply too risky and is a recipe for disaster.

You have to analyze and offer your affiliates several business opportunities to help them succeed. This is your task as a leader. Your affiliates will have the choice to start with one business opportunity or can join several other opportunities to create multiple streams of high cash flow residual income streams. The success formula in MLM business is:

Well Researched Business Opportunities + Network Marketing System = Exponential Income

Features of a Network Marketing System

The features of a successful **Network Marketing System** that will give you and your team the '**X**' **Factor** to sponsor more leaders in your organization are enumerated below:

- Replicating Marketing Funnel for Your Business and Affiliates

- Professional Grade Auto-responder for your marketing funnel, fully controlled by you

- Marketing Dashboard with Analytics to manage your advertising campaigns

- Viral Blogging System (SEO Optimized) that will drive free traffic to your website and lead capture pages

- Social Media Integration

- Training Videos for Operating the Marketing System

- Training Videos for generating website traffic and building leadership in your team that is crucial for your success

- State-of-the-art back office to run your business

- One-Click prospect follow up

- Appointment Scheduler

- Integrated Skype Calling

- Desktop Alert Pop-Up Tool

- Web-Based and Smartphone-Ready

- Full Technical Support for the Marketing System

- Choice of fully researched lifestyle and high cash flow business opportunities that will help you create multiple streams of residual income

- Affiliate programs that will create additional revenue streams and residual income to fund your marketing costs

It will cost you effort and thousands of dollars to create a branded marketing funnel system with personal written emails and video presentations. It will also take a substantial amount of money in developing the state of the art marketing, duplication and contact management and training systems.

In order to succeed and set up a lifestyle network marketing business you will either need to create these systems yourself or join a team /leader who have set up the systems for you.

If you don't have access to an integrated business system incorporating all the features described above, your chances of success are minimal.

You can **Click Here** to view one of the systems that is fully operational using all the concepts explained above. Alternately, you can Google and find resources to build a network marketing system from scratch. There are several resources available and you can select the best suited for your purpose. It will take you time, effort and money to build such system from the scratch but it will be worth your effort, because without a system, your chances of success are zilch.

Take Action

This book has explained to you in detail how to set up a lifestyle network marketing business from scratch. No guru will tell you his trade secrets because they want you to be followers rather than becoming a leader in your own right. The best system to join or create is to build leadership in your team.

One of the fundamental principles of wealth creation is to take **ACTION**. If you have all the knowledge in the world and take no action then NOTHING will happen. This moment will sink into eternity.

If you liked the book and gained some knowledge that will be useful to you in life, then please leave an honest review to help others find this book. It will be a small effort on your part, but an act of charity that may help in changing few lives for the better. We thank you in advance for your help.

This book is about fundamental principles of wealth creation that can be applied to any business or investing strategy. At Wealth Creation Academy, we teach multitude ways to generate passive income, which includes: real estate investing, digital publishing, affiliate marketing, multi-level marketing and investing in forex, commodities, and shares by copying experienced traders that need very little of time. You may like to get started with some of the strategies depending on your budget and time.

Other Books by the Authors

Praveen Kumar has authored several bestselling books. Please visit his website **http://praveenkumarauthor.com/** for more information

About the Authors

Praveen Kumar was abandoned by his father at the age of fourteen and joined the Navy at tender age of fifteen where education, roof and free food were guaranteed.

In order to understand the root cause of suffering he turned towards philosophy and religion. After 10 years of soul searching and meditation he understood that 'life is 'and material and spiritual world are closely interwoven. You cannot live in one without the other.

Praveen was highly successful in the Navy, where he successfully commanded submarines, sailed around the world in a yacht and received gallantry award for his contribution to the Navy.

Despite his success in the Navy, Praveen realized that lack of financial security for his family was one of key root causes of his suffering, resulting from his childhood deprivation. To improve his financial standing, Praveen took pre-mature retirement from the Navy to build his financial future through investing in Real Estate. The decision to educate on financial matters paid off, and today he and his wife are comfortably retired on six-figure passive income.

His aim is to help others create wealth in an enlightened way and empower them to live a healthy and happy life. He dedicates his time to write books and articles on financial and spiritual matters.

Prashant graduated with distinction from Auckland University as a computer engineer and later completed his MBA from the world's leading institution - INSEAD. During his successful corporate career, he worked for the most reputable consulting firms in the world - BCG & Deloitte - and represented New Zealand on Prime

Minister-led trade missions to South East Asian countries.

After successfully generating income through his passive investments in property and stocks, Prashant decided to team up with his father to help people transform their lives through the leverage of financial education.

Their website http://wealth-creation-academy.com/ is devoted to teaching people how to create Multiple Streams of Passive Income through investing in real estate, online marketing and creating digital products

www.ingramcontent.com/pod-product-compliance
Lightning Source LLC
Chambersburg PA
CBHW020845210326
41598CB00019B/1977